VISUAL
GEOGRAPHY
SERIES

RUSSIA
in pictures

Prepared by Galina Klimenko

STERLING
PUBLISHING CO., INC.
NEW YORK

Oak Tree Press Co., Ltd.
London & Sydney

VISUAL GEOGRAPHY SERIES

This is the Dnieper hydro-electric power station in Zaporozhye, in the Ukraine, one of hundreds of Russian power plants and stations.

ACKNOWLEDGMENTS
The author and publishers wish to thank Mr. Nicholas Dani-
loff for his invaluable advice and assistance in the preparation
of the manuscript, and the Novosti Press Agency, Moscow,
and the Tass Agency, Moscow, for their aid in obtaining photographs. The publishers also wish to thank Louisa Bumagin
Hellegers for the use of additional photographs.

Twelfth Printing, 1979
Copyright © 1979, 1977, 1976, 1975, 1974, 1973, 1972, 1971, 1970, 1967, 1966
by Sterling Publishing Co., Inc.
Two Park Avenue, New York, N.Y. 10016
Distributed in Australia by Oak Tree Press Co., Ltd.,
P.O. Box J34, Brickfield Hill, Sydney 2000, N.S.W.
Distributed in the United Kingdom
by Ward Lock Ltd., 116 Baker Street, London W 1
Manufactured in the United States of America   *All rights reserved*
Library of Congress Catalog Card No.: 66-25201
Sterling ISBN 0-8069-1072-0 Trade   Oak Tree 7061-6032 0
1073-9 Library

CONTENTS

INDEX

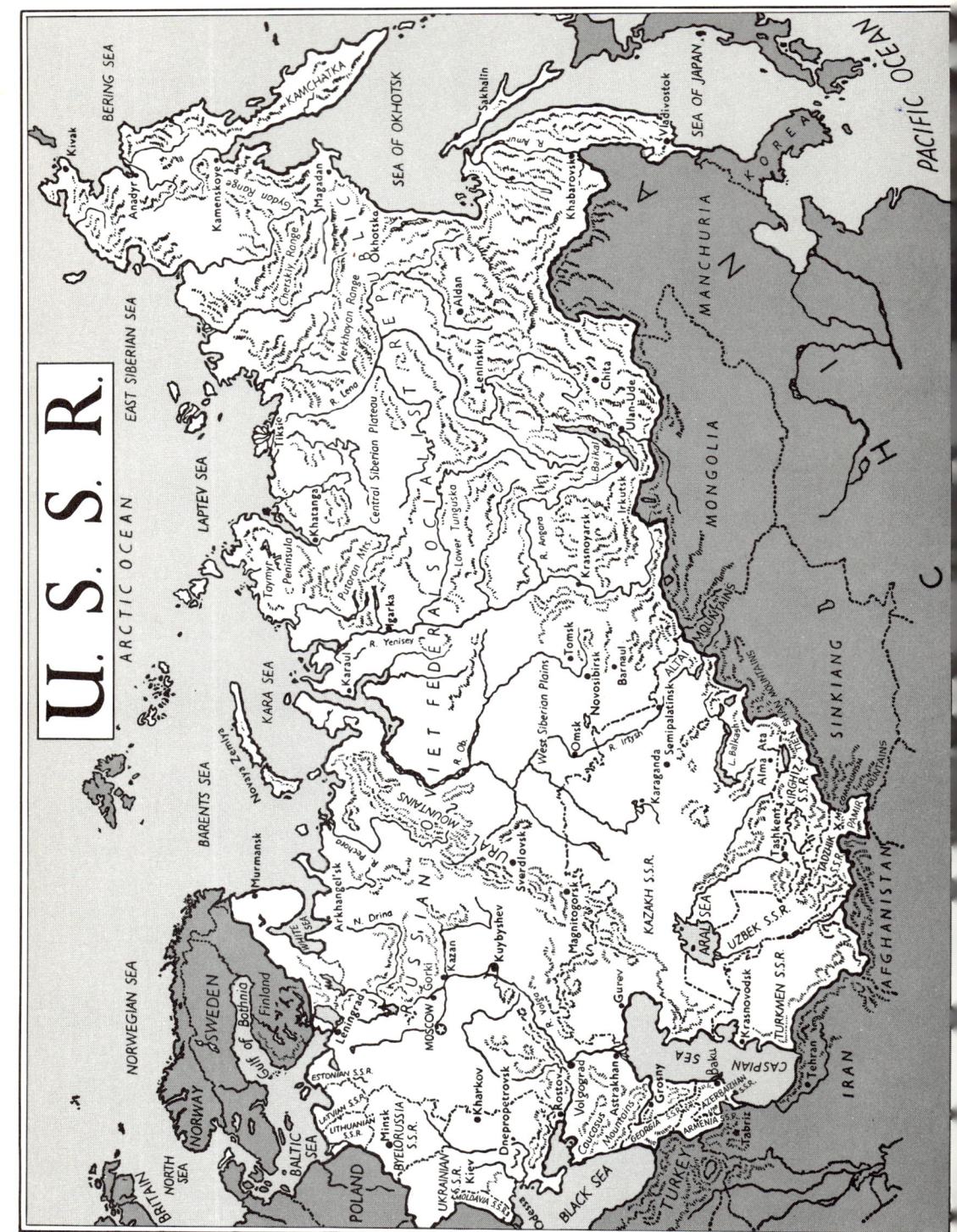

Red Square. Moscow, the capital of the USSR, is a truly unique city for it manages to combine the urban with the rural, a perfect blend of the country and a busy, bustling metropolis. It is one of the few cities in the world not yet seriously affected by the problem of air pollution.

I. THE LAND

THE NAME RUSSIA was generally used to refer to the land that composed the Russian Empire before 1917, when the Russian Revolution occurred and subsequently led to the establishing of the Union of Soviet Socialist Republics (USSR). Today, outsiders continue to refer to the whole of the USSR as Russia, although within the Soviet Union the name is confined to the largest and most prominent of the USSR's 15 republics—the Russian Soviet Federated Socialist Republic (RSFSR). This republic, containing close to half the total population of the USSR, all but approximately 2,000,000 square miles of the USSR's territory, and many of the nation's most important cities (including the capital, Moscow), is naturally much more familiar to the Western world than are the other, less influential, 14 republics: Estonia, Latvia, Lithuania, Byelorussia, Ukraine and Moldavia, along the Western border; Georgia, Armenia, and Azerbaijan between the Black and Caspian Seas in Transcaucasia; and the Kazakh, Turkmen, Uzbek, Tadzhik and Kirghiz Republics in Central Asia.

Minsk, the capital of Byelorussia, was founded in the beginning of the 11th century, and is one of the cultural hubs of the Soviet Union.

AREA AND POPULATION

The USSR is the largest country in the world. Covering some 8,647,250 square miles, it is over twice as big as China, or the United States (with Hawaii and Alaska) and seven times as large as India. Included within its boundaries is roughly one-sixth of the earth's land area, and its vast bulk extends over two continents: Europe and Asia.

Except in the west, where it borders on Norway, Finland, Poland, Czechoslovakia, Hungary and Rumania, the USSR's boundaries are for the most part formed by natural marine and mountain barriers. Reaching from the Arctic Ocean (in the north) to the Black Sea and the boundaries of Turkey, Iran, Afghanistan, China, Mongolia and Korea (in the south), the USSR extends from its most western point on the shores of the Baltic Sea all the way to the Pacific Ocean. In its most northeastern corner, the USSR is separated from Alaska by the 52-mile-wide Bering Strait.

In the 18th century, Russian geographers created a purely arbitrary separation of Russia into what are today known as European Russia and Asian Russia, using the Ural Mountains as a dividing line. Stretching for 1,300 miles from the Kara Sea in the north to the Caspian Sea in the south, the Ural Mountains are by no means a natural boundary or barrier, since they rise to an altitude of no more than 5,560 feet; even the soil and vegetation on both sides of the Urals are identical. Nevertheless, this geographical separation of the USSR has endured.

The Soviet Union has the third largest population in the world, after China and India. In 1979, the population approximated 258,000,000, with almost half the people widely scattered in rural areas. Throughout the USSR's enormous territory are scattered some 1,763 towns and over 3,255 urban communities, including several cities founded over 1,000 years ago.

There are 14 cities with 1,000,000 inhabitants or more: Moscow, 7,820,000; Leningrad, 4,425,000; Kiev, 2,080,000; Tashkent, 1,643,000; Baku, 1,406,000; Kharkov,

The Cathedral of St. Sophia in Kiev is an architectural monument, built about 1037. It is one of the many fine examples of early Russian architecture.

1,385,000; Gorky, 1,305,000; Novosibirsk, 1,286,000; Kuibyshev, 1,186,000; Sverdlovsk, 1,171,000; Minsk, 1,189,000; Tbilisi, 1,030,000; Odessa, 1,023,000; and Omsk, 1,002,000.

A land of many cultures, the USSR is composed of more than 100 different nationalities and ethnic groups, though three-fourths of the population are Eastern Slavs (Russians, Ukrainians and Byelorussians). Tremendously heavy casualties among the male population in World War II resulted in a disproportion of 55 females to 45 males for every 100 people.

Like many of the other Baltic cities, Tallin, Estonia, resembles the towns of Western Europe, with its narrow streets and peaked roofs.

Famous for its shashlyk and high-speed boats (better known as "gliders"), Lake Ritsa in Georgia is one of the USSR's most popular vacation resorts.

Traffic is still fairly light by most western standards, even here on Gorki Street in Moscow. Moscow's streets are enormously wide, and pedestrians cross at some points by means of underpasses. This allows traffic to move at high speeds. Left turns are made in outlined areas in the middle of blocks instead of at intersections.

A camel caravan crosses a fragile bridge over the roaring waters of the Vanch River, high in the Pamir Mountains of Soviet Central Asia.

The Crimea, the most magnificent peninsula of the USSR, can be explored along the "goat paths" of the past.

9

Gurzuf is one of the most picturesque health resorts on the coast of the Crimean Peninsula. The mountain in the background is called Medved (or Bear) Mountain. Legend has it that a bear came down to the sea for a drink of water and was turned to stone.

TOPOGRAPHY

Despite the popular Western belief that the USSR is for the most part a flat and level land, more than one-third of its territory consists of plateaus and mountain ranges. However, broad plains and lowlands do predominate in the western areas. The land mass west of the Urals and north of the Caucasus Mountains up to the Vistula River is occupied almost entirely by the East European (Russian) Plain, while on the eastern side of the Urals stretches the immense West Siberian Plain. It has often been said that the patience and endurance of the Russian people came from the monotony of the infinite plain and its harsh, severe climate.

Elevations, plateaus and mountains are found primarily in the eastern part of the USSR. Extending eastwards from the Yenisei River to the Lena River, the area of the Central Siberian Plateau alone is equal to half that of Western Europe. Many rugged mountain chains are scattered throughout Far Eastern Siberia. In

This is one of the 20 geysers found on the Kamchatka Peninsula, which has over 60 active volcanoes. It spurts steam and water out of the ground to a height of nearly 300 feet.

Situated on the sub-tropical southern coast of the Crimea, the small village of Yalta grew to become a world-famous seaside resort. In 1945 it was the site of the historic Yalta Conference between Roosevelt, Churchill and Stalin.

the south, the Central Asian deserts border on the Tien Shan and Altai Mountains. The Pamir Mountains border on China. Between the Black and Caspian Seas is the tallest peak in all of Europe, Mt. Elbrus (18,481 feet), part of the Caucasus mountain barrier.

VEGETATION ZONES

The land mass of the USSR is divided by latitude into several broad strips, differing from each other in climate, vegetation and soil, as well as in flora and fauna. Also referred to as vegetation zones, they are (north to south): the tundra, the forest, the steppes and the desert.

THE TUNDRA

The tundra, a permafrost (permanently frozen) area stretching along the shores of the Arctic Ocean and the Arctic Islands, is a bleak unforested region of frozen wasteland, sparsely dotted with patches of moss, lichen and occasional bushes and dwarf trees. Its widest point is at the Kara Sea in northern Siberia. On the Kamchatka Peninsula, desolate, gloomy marshes reach southward to a latitude of about 60° N. The few shrubs capable of surviving the fierce climate grow in tangled, protective clusters. Despite the below-freezing temperatures, in the summer the land becomes marshy and swarms with mosquitoes.

THE FOREST

Immediately south of the tundra, covering nearly half the territory of the USSR, sprawls the dense forest zone. Its southern frontiers ex-

Creating fascinating silhouettes against the sand are the "trees on stilted roots" near Lake Baikal's Peschanaya Bay.

Overlooking the beautiful Black Sea is this romantic "Swallows' Nest" castle, built on a sheer cliff in the Crimea.

tend eastward to the Altai Mountains approximately to the line of the cities of Orel, Kiev, and Kazan. Almost every species of tree imaginable grows somewhere in this enormous 4,240,000-square-mile area. There are boundless forests in Siberia, where the chief species are pine, fir and cedar. This is the famous *taiga*, its untrod, virgin forests stretching for hundreds of miles. Further south are the beautiful silver birch, pine, oak, maple, linden, fir, cedar, and spruce trees, so typical of the Russian landscape. Hidden below the picturesque bushes of aromatic wild berries, the floor of the forest displays an unlimited variety of mushrooms, offering the inhabitants an opportunity to go mushroom- and berry-picking, a popular traditional pastime.

THE STEPPES

The steppe zone is preceded by a relatively narrow section of land known as the "forest steppe," where the transition between the forests of the north and the steppes (plains) of the south takes place. In this narrow strip, large masses of forests alternate with great open spaces. Grey forest soil predominates, mixed with the *chernozem* (black earth) which extends far into the steppe zone.

The steppes themselves are ocean-like grass expanses that offer the best natural conditions for agriculture, and this area is referred to as the "breadbasket of the USSR." The rich black earth would ensure unusually high crop yields were it not for poor agricultural management, lack of modern farm equipment, and frequent bad weather. (During World War II, the German occupational forces exported this soil to their own country by the trainloads.)

The steppes are covered by a wide variety of tough feather grasses tall enough to hide a man on horseback. Trees are rare, but tulips, hyacinths, stars of Bethlehem and many other flowers sprinkle the fields of the steppes with an array of hues.

This section of the country has played a vital part in the culture and history of Russia. Poets and writers have found great inspirations in the overpowering vastness of the steppes, often comparing them to the sea, their tranquil surface producing the illusion of waves at the slightest indication of wind. All throughout early history, the Russians lived in constant fear of nomadic invaders crossing the open, unprotected steppes, which provided easy access to the rest of Russia.

THE DESERT

From the southeastern corner of the Russian Plain, on the north shore of the Caspian Sea, a vast desert region extends eastwards, taking in Kazakhstan, Turkmenia, Uzbekistan and western Kirghizia. Though sandy deserts predominate, small areas of stony desert exist as well.

THE SUB-TROPICS

A narrow coastal strip along the Black Sea, including the Crimean Peninsula, does not belong to the four major belts of climate, and its distinctive sub-tropical features are not found anywhere else in the USSR. Its mineral springs are famous for their exceptional cures; the air is fresh, and unusually invigorating. The coastal hills are covered with luxuriant flora. Vines climb up rocky cliffs above the azure sea, while the flamboyant Riviera-like coast is covered with magnolia, eucalyptus, and hibiscus.

The Yashil-Kul Lake in the Pamir Mountains is situated 9,842 feet above sea level. The Pamirs boast the highest (24,390 feet) mountain in all the USSR, Mt. Communism.

The search for food in the frozen wasteland of the tundra occupies most of the reindeer's long day.

FAUNA

Polar bears, foxes, lemmings and reindeer roam the icy, windswept tundra. The Soviet Union's vast forests abound in fur-bearing animals (from squirrels to sables, and muskrat to mink), along with brown bears, deer, and wolves. In the Far Eastern areas live tigers, panthers and snow leopards or ounces.

The tall, weaving grasses of the steppes provide great security for small animals such as hamsters, marmots and mice, while the arid desert region is a paradise for lizards, tortoises, snakes, gazelles, antelopes, and barkhan cats. Porcupines and wild boars flourish in the subtropics.

Perhaps the most famous Russian animal is the Borzoi (wolfhound). Formerly dogs of state for the Czars, the elegant, fleet wolfhounds were used to chase and catch wolves on the steppes.

Slightly camera-shy, this little sable has a cool retreat which serves as a convenient hiding place.

"Ferocious" bears figure prominently in almost all Russian fairy tales. Having a friendly row, these two Moscow zoo tenants do not appear to be homesick for their more natural habitat in the Arctic.

RIVERS, LAKES AND SEAS

Magnificent and mighty rivers flow on both sides of the Urals, serving the USSR as traffic arteries for barges and boats of every kind. With tributaries too numerous to mention, these broad, slow rivers flow through the enormous plains, providing the farmlands with life-giving moisture. In no other country are there so many inland waterways.

Originating in the marshes, the rivers have been the main roads of Russian history, for

Some believe that Vladimir I. Ulyanov adopted his pen name, Lenin, from this Siberian river, the Lena, after he spent several years in exile in Siberia. Recently, large deposits of diamonds were discovered in Siberia, making the USSR, already rich in minerals, including gold, iron and coal, the leading country in unmined diamond reserves.

Spanning the Moscow River are a number of bridges including the Novo-Arbat Bridge. Against the skyline stands the Ukraine Hotel, an example of the overdecorated, pompous, heavy architecture of the Stalinist period. Now, for the first time, Russian architects have begun to experiment with steel, glass and concrete, with exciting results, promising to make Moscow a much more modern metropolis.

along their banks moved the early tide of Russian colonization. For centuries, the rivers were almost the only means of communication, and even today they serve the USSR well. Early in Russian history, the rivers were connected by means of "portages"—light boats were carried from one waterway to the next.

The Dniester, the Don, the Dnieper, the Volga, the Ob, the Lena, the Yenisei, the Irtysh, the Pechora and the Angara are the chief rivers of the USSR. Today, these rivers are connected by a system of artificial canals which are used for both transportation and irrigation purposes, the most important being the White Sea-Baltic Canal, the Moscow-Volga Canal, the Volga-Don Canal and the Volga-Baltic Waterway.

The Volga, often referred to as "Mother Volga," flows southwards for 2,290 miles and empties into the Caspian Sea. This mighty river

Peterhof, near Leningrad, was the country residence of Peter the Great. Laid out in classic French style with formal gardens and watercourses, it is now a public park. Its fountains come from natural springs—there is even a children's park where jets of water rise unexpectedly when the youngsters walk over certain pebble-strewn areas!

The oldest means of transportation in history is still the most popular: walking. This may be due to the Russian's desire for physical fitness, but it is also often attributed to the crowded apartments.
Here is a view of the footbridge across the Dnieper River.

Leningrad (St. Petersburg), founded in 1703 by Peter the Great, is undoubtedly the most beautiful city in the Soviet Union. The classic palaces and monuments, the picturesque squares and the layout of the broad, tree-lined streets were the work of famous Italian architects.

The Kremlin, a fortress in mediæval times, contains a museum, a treasure house of Russian art and craftsmanship. It encloses within its walls the cultural, religious and the political history of Russia.

has for centuries captured the hearts of the Russians, and although many of the rivers are spoken of affectionately by the people, the Volga is most commemorated in songs, poems and legends.

Among the USSR's many lakes is Lake Baikal in Siberia, the deepest lake in the world and the largest in Asia and Europe. Situated east of the Volga River is the famous salt-water lake, Baskunchak, better known as "Russia's salt-cellar." It is continually fed by many salt springs. Though salt extractions have been carried on for over a century, its reserves of common salt appear to be inexhaustible. According to Soviet scientists, the lake's supply of salt could last the world for more than a thousand years.

Of primary importance is the Baltic Sea, offering ships the shortest route to the Atlantic Ocean. The Caspian Sea, the chief source of the world-renowned beluga caviar, is the largest inland body of water in the world. The USSR has access to many other seas as well. Most of them, however, are covered with ice for a good

part of the year, making navigation almost impossible. The ports of Odessa on the Black Sea, Kaliningrad and Klaipeda on the Baltic, and Murmansk on the Arctic Ocean, are the only ports which are not icebound in the winter.

CLIMATE

The climate of European USSR is for the most part "continental," characterized by hot but relatively short summers, and long, extremely cold winters. Accompanied by heavy snowfall and blizzards, the winter months are harsh. There is little time for the farmer to plant and harvest his crop during the brief summer season.

In the southern part of the USSR, the snow cover lasts from 40 to 60 days, while in the extreme northeastern portion of the USSR it may remain for as long as 260 days, often with temperatures of $-5°$ F. and lower. The world's coldest inhabited place is Oymyakon, in Eastern Siberia, where a temperature of $-96°$ F. has been registered. The Purga, an intense blizzard bringing up to 100-mile-per-hour winds mixed

(Right) The graceful Spasskaya Tower is the tallest of the 20 towers of the Kremlin wall.

(Left) An ancient town, founded in the late 12th century, the city of Riga, Latvia, was built at the crossing of important land and sea trade routes. This is a square in the old part of the city.

Recently most of Moscow's streets have been widened a great deal by moving back virtually whole blocks of buildings. Here, a statue of Apollo overlooks Sverdlov Square from the top of the Bolshoi Theatre.

The USSR spends nearly 15,000,000 rubles annually on the physical education of children alone. Many in Russia do exercises each morning to the instructions on the radio. For a few minutes every day the nation is "all together now, one, two, three . . ." This mountain skating rink is located in Medeo near Alma-Ata.

with snow, blows over the enormous plains of the USSR. On the other hand, the thermometers of Central Asia have been known to register temperatures of 120 to 130° F. during the summer months.

The Crimea's southern coast and Transcaucasia have a sub-tropical climate similar to that of the Mediterranean. This is due not only to the closeness of the sea and the low altitudes, but also to the high mountain barrier in the north, which serves as a wall against the cold air. A truly beautiful region, this was a popular resort area for the Czars and other notables, and was sometimes described as "the Russian Riviera."

NATURAL RESOURCES

Russia would be practically self-sufficient, were it not for the lack of a few raw materials such as rubber, tin and some tropical crops. Since the USSR possesses about one-fifth of the world's forest land, the annual natural increase of its trees is sufficient to meet the timber requirements of every country on earth.

Its numerous rivers make the USSR first in the world in water-power resources. The potential hydro-electric generating capacity amounts to almost 300,000,000 kilowatts.

Astounding reserves of copper and about half the world's supply of iron ore appear to exist in the USSR, while Russian coal resources are superseded only by those of the United States. Estimated to have as much as 60 per cent of the world's total oil, the USSR is also rich in reserves of natural gas.

Other valuable minerals include silver, gold, diamonds, manganese, lead, zinc, salt, nickel, bauxite, tungsten, mercury, and sulphur, plus the widest variety of metals to be found anywhere in the world.

The development of Siberia's resources is a main goal of Russian planners. By 1975, the oil fields of western Siberia had begun to replace those of Baku as Russia's chief petroleum-producing area. Spurring Russia's development of its vast northern Asian region is tension with China, expressed in border clashes in recent years.

Tashkent, the capital of the Uzbek Republic, was founded sometime in the 7th century B.C. It received its Turkish name (Stone City) in the 12th century A.D., and in 1865 was captured by the Russians. Today Novoi Street is the main thoroughfare of Tashkent, with modern buildings rising next to magnificent monuments of the past. Unfortunately, much of the ancient architecture was heavily damaged by the earthquakes of 1966.

2. HISTORY

ALTHOUGH IT IS BELIEVED that Russia was inhabited by man as early as the Stone Age, traditionally Russian history is regarded as beginning with the foundation of the Kievan State in A.D. 862. However, according to the records left by the Greek historian, Herodotus, the southern part of Russia (the steppe zone) was inhabited by a people called Scythians in the 5th century B.C. Russia's exposed steppes were an irresistible temptation to potential invaders. Impossible to protect, the steppes were the country's Achilles heel, resulting in much of Russia's turbulent early history.

In the 3rd century B.C., the Scythians were displaced by a distantly related tribe, the Sarmatians, who occupied the vulnerable southern steppe until the 3rd century A.D. After they conquered the Sarmatians in the same century, the German Goths were devastated by a fierce Mongolian tribe of Huns within a few short years. The 6th century brought an invasion by the Turkish Avars; the 7th century brought the powerful Khazars, who conquered the Slavs and settled in the south; and the 8th century saw the establishment of the Bulgars in the Volga region.

Note: Russia followed the Julian calendar up until the Revolution of 1917, and by the 19th century this calendar had fallen behind the Western Gregorian calendar by 13 days. All dates mentioned prior to 1917 are given by the Julian calendar to avoid confusion. Thus, for example, the Bolshevik Revolution occurred on October 25, 1917 according to the Gregorian calendar, rather than November 7. After 1917 the USSR adopted the Gregorian calendar used elsewhere throughout the world.

Armenian history originated in the 9th century B.C. *in the state of Urartu. Recent excavations show that Urartu had a highly advanced agricultural and commercial civilization. Armenia abounds in the most magnificent marble, with varied hues of amber, grey, black with gold veins, and the beautiful tufa. Here is an ancient Kurd cemetery at the foot of the Alagez Mountains in Armenia.*

THE SLAVS

Russia's early recorded history took place in the western part of European Russia. Because only scant information has been preserved, the origin of the so-called Eastern Slavs is still being disputed today, though many historians believe that the Slavs first appeared in the Polish marshes of Galicia. Their ancestors are presumed to have been the Neolithic tribes which inhabited this area several centuries prior to the Christian era. The early Slavs lived scattered throughout the territory in small tribes. Although no one unifying Slavic language existed, the tribal dialects of the Slavs apparently had a common origin. The Eastern Slavs, having somehow managed to survive numerous nomadic invasions, were by the 9th century well established both in the north and south.

THE KHAZARS

Though conquered by the Khazars, the Slavs enjoyed a great deal of freedom under their tolerant domination, and were able to engage in intensive trade with the Eastern Arabs. They had to pay tribute to the Khazars, but the Slavs were allowed to settle wherever they pleased, and they erected many important trade towns, such as Kiev and Novgorod, along the rivers. By connecting the rivers into a north-south route from the Gulf of Finland to the Black Sea, the Eastern Slavs were able to trade with Constantinople. Their flourishing trade soon attracted the attention of the Varangians, Scandinavian warriors and traders, who were also interested in the Greek markets. The Slavs and the Varangians made a mutual trade agreement, the Varangians promising to protect the trade routes.

THE KIEVAN STATE (9th-13th centuries)

Very few records have survived about the founder of the Varangian dynasty, Rurik. According to the chronicles, the people of Novgorod managed to expel the powerful Varangians in 862, only to find almost immediately that they could not do without them. Chaos and instability prevailed—the Slavic tribes, unable to settle their differences, were constantly feuding. To return order to the land, the Slavic tribes invited the Varangians to "come and rule over us and our wide land." Rurik arrived in Novgorod in 862 and established himself there as "ruler." From this time onward, the name Rus was associated with the Eastern Slavs and became the name of the

Kirghizia's "useful" land consists almost entirely of cultivated meadows and pastures. This mountainous region was settled by Mongol Tartars even before the 13th century.

Silhouetted against the open sky are ancient family burial vaults in Kirghizia.

Founded in the 3rd century A.D., *Sudak belonged to the Genoese in the Middle Ages. Here they built a fortress so sturdy that it is well preserved to this day.*

country. The origin of the word Rus is still being disputed today. Some historians contend that it was the name of one of the Varangian tribes, while others insist that it was used in the southern steppes long before the time of Rurik.

Oleg, the kinsman and successor of Rurik, merged the Eastern Slavs of the north and south into a single Kievan State under the rule of the Varangians, by transferring the capital to Kiev after freeing that territory from its Khazar domination.

Under the rule of Prince Vladimir I (980–1015), a line of strong fortification was built to fend off the ever-increasing attacks by aggressive nomads. Vladimir accepted the Greek Orthodox rite, making Christianity the state religion. Although he frequently resorted to the use of force in order to convert the heathen natives, Prince Vladimir was later made a saint.

Christianity brought with it the cultural influences of Byzantium (Constantinople), then the capital of the declining Roman Empire. The Russians quickly adopted the use of stone rather than wood in the building of churches, following the Greek example. They soon developed a distinctly Russian architectural style, however, and achieved great beauty in icons (portraits, especially of Christ), an art form which also originated in Greece. By the 11th century, Russian local customary law had been codified and the Cyrillic alphabet adopted.

The decline of the Kievan State began with the death of Yaroslav the Wise (1019–54). When first founded, the Kievan State was ruled in succession by one of the princes of the dynasty, and for as long as the family remained small, the power was concentrated. Yaroslav, on the other hand, willed that his realm be divided among his sons. Thereafter, the country became more divided with each new generation, since each prince considered his principality the exclusive property of his family. The political importance and authority of the Kievan Prince declined, shifting from Kiev to the western and northern principalities. In 1169, Kiev itself was besieged and sacked by another Russian, Prince Andrei Bogolubski of Suzdal, who then made the city of Vladimir, on the river Klyazma, the capital of the so-called "grand duchy."

The city of Samarkand dates back to the 4th century B.C. *Destroyed by Alexander the Great in 329* B.C., *and then again by Genghis Khan in* A.D. *1220, later on it became the capital of Tamerlane's empire. The tomb and palace of Tamerlane are among the many monuments of ancient and mediæval architecture left there. Today it is one of the major cultural and economic cities of Central Asia.*

THE TARTAR INVASION

Kiev's final downfall came with the invasion of the Mongol Tartars from Asia in 1237–40, one of the greatest disasters in all of Russia's history. More than half the population were massacred; the rest either were led into captivity or fled to the forests. Kiev was almost totally destroyed, its churches razed to the ground. The work, the art, and the culture of nearly 300 years went up in smoke. Only Pskov and Novgorod and its northern provinces were spared.

THE TARTAR YOKE (13th-15th centuries)

Khan Batu, the Tartar leader, established the empire of the Golden Horde in the south and east of Russia, on the Volga River. This empire lasted until 1480. For over 200 years the Rus-

sian nation was bled white by the Tartars, but the most horrifying aspect of their rule was their periodic attacks upon the Russian people, when whole regions were depopulated overnight.

One of the vital consequences of the Tartar occupation was that the country was divided into two parts, southwestern and northeastern. Thereafter, Russia's economic and political life was focussed in the northeast, with Tver as the political hub. Although still paying taxes to the Golden Horde, the Muscovite princes of the grand duchy of Vladimir regained some of their power and concentrated on unifying their political position.

The beautiful Assumption Cathedral in Karelia, the area adjoining Finland, is one of the finest examples of Russia's early wood architecture. It was erected in the 13th or 14th century, and in spite of its age is still in good condition. Many of the early wooden structures were totally destroyed during the numerous invasions that Karelia suffered.

The Kremlin Palace at the end of the 17th century. The city of Moscow itself and its fortifications have been rebuilt many times because of the frequent, devastating fires that the city suffered.

THE MOSCOW STATE
(12th-17th centuries)

Liberation of Eastern Russia from the Tartars came about with the rise of Moscow. During the 12th and 13th centuries, when the principality of Suzdal-Vladimir was at the height of its power, Moscow was but a tiny fortified village under its jurisdiction. Because the rulers of Vladimir possessed the title of Grand Duke, all the other princes recognized them as their sovereigns.

Moscow grew, for several reasons. It was to Moscow that Metropolitan Peter, the head of the Russian Church, had eventually moved his residence after the fall of Kiev. Also, the location of Moscow at the crossing of the old trade routes was advantageous, for it was in an area not easily accessible to outside attacks by nomads.

During the reign of Dmitri Donskoi (1359–89), Moscow's importance steadily increased. Prince Donskoi's refusal to pay tribute to the Tartars in 1380 resulted in a great battle at Kulikovo Field. Here the Tartars were defeated, and though the Golden Horde was not wiped out, it was sufficiently weakened so that it never was able to raise its head again. By 1480, the Tartar power had completely fallen apart.

The last three decades of the 15th century were years of tremendous expansion for the Moscow State. Ivan III (reign 1462–1505) added four areas, Tver, Novgorod, Rostov and Vyatka, to the grand duchy, thereby ruling one of the biggest territorial states in all of Europe. Under the direction of Ivan III (called Ivan the Great), Moscow gained the appearance of a capital, with beautiful churches and rich, magnificent palaces. In 1493, Ivan III adopted the title of "Sovereign of all Russia." The 16th century was devoted to the difficult task of uniting the country.

IVAN IV, THE TERRIBLE (1533-84)

Under Vasily III, the boyars, who were the upper class nobility, had grown ambitious and they became exceedingly difficult to control. With the advent of Ivan IV to the throne in 1533, an onslaught against the boyars began. Ivan created the "Oprichina," a military police force, with which he exterminated the undesirable elements of the aristocracy, and confiscated the boyars' land holdings, distributing them among his hired assassins.

Conquering the Tartar khanates of Kazan and Astrakhan, Ivan the Terrible added another huge area, the lower and the middle Volga to Russia. The annexation and colonization of Siberia began in the 16th century, after its conqueror, the Cossack Timofeievich Yermak, made a present of the Siberian kingdom to Ivan IV. The Cossacks were communities of soldier-peasants that had grown up on the frontier with the Tartar states.

In a magnificent ceremony, Ivan IV had himself crowned in 1547 and assumed the title of Czar (Caesar). Much concerned with increasing the prestige of the crown, and realizing that Moscow could not compare with the Western capitals in culture, education or brilliance, Ivan IV sought to improve the economic conditions of the country through trade and closer contact with Europe.

SERFDOM

Theoretically, both the land-owner and the peasant were considered "serfs," each obliged to serve the state in his way, the land-owner by fighting, the peasant by providing for him.

But in time the land-owners came to look upon the peasants as their own personal slaves. Under Ivan IV, as compensation for being deprived of their political influence, the land-owners were given land grants as well as increased rights over the peasants. With pressing military needs, the land-owners began restricting the freedom of the peasants. By the end of the 16th century, the process of turning the peasants into serfs was complete.

Due to Ivan the Terrible's Oprichina, the economic problems, and the enslavement of the peasants, the country entered into "The Time of Troubles"—1584–1613. It was during the beginning of this period that Boris Godunov, a boyar, became regent. In 1593, he was reluctantly elected Czar and was faced immediately with the intrigues and jealousies of other boyar families. He died suddenly in 1605. During this unsettled period, peasant uprisings, civil war, lack of authority, and invasions by Swedes, Poles and Cossacks added to the chaos. Finally, after the Polish armies were driven out, some degree of order was restored. Michael F. Romanov, a boyar, was chosen as the new Czar on February 21, 1613. Thus began the Romanov Dynasty.

Bogdan Z. Khmelnitsky (1593–1657), a Cossack and sovereign of the Ukraine, ended the Ukraine's aspirations for independence by asking for an alliance with Russia against the Poles and swearing allegiance to the Czar in 1654.

THE RUSSIAN EMPIRE

Because Russia was surrounded on three sides by enemies, for centuries its main concern was that of defence, and this served to dictate foreign policy. Despite great territorial gains, the country, lacking a stable military and administrative structure, grew internally weaker.

PETER THE GREAT (1689-1725)

Peter I, who became Czar in 1689, had a dynamic personality. His novel concept of governing the country gave Russia a new political position and prestige among the nations of Europe. Being acutely aware of Russia's deficiencies, and weaknesses, he used the state as a "whip," or driving force, to strengthen and "Westernize" the country and its people. His radical policies provoked strong resistance at home among his subjects, who were accustomed to passive administrations.

Peter I was extremely devoted to his people, but being an impatient man, he drove them, as well as himself, mercilessly. Assuming the title of "Emperor," he proceeded to impose a series of reforms by force on his "idle and ignorant subjects." He was responsible for the creation of a regular army and navy, for improvement in state government departments, and the formation of a Senate and various

The throne of Boris Godunov. Reluctantly elected Czar in 1598, he died in 1605, and was immortalized in the 1869 opera, "Boris Godunov" by Modest P. Musorgsky.

Ministries. The Church was "decapitated" and made a mere governmental department, subordinated directly to the Czar. The fiscal system was revised; education and culture were made compulsory for the children of the nobility; and modern industries, based on European methods, were first introduced into Russia.

Seeking outlets to the sea, Peter acquired Estonia, Livonia, Ingermanland, Finland and areas of Karelia after 20 years of struggle in the Great Northern War. Thus, Peter gained the long-desired access to the Baltic. To symbolize the beginning of a new European era for Russia, in 1703 he erected a city in his own name—St. Petersburg—on the Gulf of Finland, and made it the new capital of Russia.

One of the oldest customs in Russia was that of exchanging eggs at Easter. Here is an example of the delicate workmanship of a crystal egg, designed in 1909 for the royal family.

Catherine the Great, a poor German princess, was married to the Russian heir-apparent, Peter III. Shortly after Peter ascended the throne, he died under very suspicious circumstances. Most historians feel that Catherine was responsible for his untimely departure.

In the next two centuries, Russia increased its territories through the Russo-Turkish Wars while participating actively in the affairs of Europe. Peter's daughter, the Empress Elizabeth (reign 1741–61) allied herself against Prussia in the Seven Years War. However, her nephew and successor Peter III, withdrew Russia from the War. Upon his unexplainable death, his wife, Catherine II, born a German princess, became the new Empress.

CATHERINE THE GREAT (1762-96)

Catherine II, who very much admired Peter the Great, followed his policy of expanding Russia's territories, making the nation a major European power. Among the large new territories she added to Russia were parts of Poland, Byelorussia, the Black Sea shore and the Ukraine west of the Dnieper River. Although under Catherine's "enlightened despotism" Russia's art and culture began to flower, her political reforms served only to consolidate the power of the crown. The privileged classes benefited, at the expense of social reforms.

ALEXANDER I (1801-25)

Under Catherine's successor, Paul I, Russia's eastward expansion reached Alaska and the North American continent. It was during the reign of Alexander I that Russia fought one of its greatest nationalistic wars, throwing back the French under Napoleon in 1812. Russians refer to this as The Patriotic War. With Napoleon's final defeat, the Congress of Vienna peace settlement made Russia and Austria the leading powers in Europe. It was at this time that Alexander I promoted a loose union of states under the name of "The Holy Alliance."

Catherine the Great was a collector of some of the most magnificent carriages in the world. This one, on display in Moscow today, was made in St. Petersburg in 1739.

The notorious Yemilian I. Pugachev claimed to be Peter III and led his followers against Catherine the Great in one of the biggest rebellions ever to shake Russia. His initial victories were short-lived, however, and on January 11, 1775, Catherine had him executed.

NICHOLAS I (1825-55)

An active revolutionary movement had originated in Russia itself, meanwhile. It culminated in the Decembrist Revolt, which was brought on by Alexander's death in 1825. Filled with liberal ideas, the Decembrists dreamed of reforming Russia according to utopian Socialism. At the confused time of the succession, the cry went out for "Konstantin and Constitution." Konstantin was one of Alexander's brothers, and the ignorant soldiers believed that Constitution was Konstantin's wife! The Decembrist revolt was put down, Konstantin abdicated, and Nicholas I came to the throne.

Nicholas felt that revolutions were the result of education and he therefore opened many institutions of higher learning, but, the curriculum was rigidly supervised by the police and by severe censorship. Nicholas gained the reputation of being the most reactionary monarch in all Europe. Russia's reputation suffered greatly during the 19th century because of his enthusiasm for suppressing revolts for other monarchs.

THE REFORMS OF ALEXANDER II (1855-81)

Russia's defeat in the Crimean War (1854–56) against England, Turkey, France and Sardinia exposed to the whole world the complete decadence of the Russian state. Nicholas I, with an army of nearly 1,000,000 men, was unable to crush the 70,000-man army of the enemy.

He was succeeded by Alexander II, who was to be one of the more liberal monarchs of Russia. The new Czar was responsible for the "Abolition of Serfdom," which took place in 1861. Although for some time many of the liberal nobles had advocated this reform, the majority feared that it would ruin the landowners economically, thus destroying the Crown's chief source of revenue and support. It soon became apparent that the peasant reforms would not live up to expectations, and the land-owners preserved a great deal of their personal power over the fate of the peasants.

In the two years that followed, there were over a thousand peasant disturbances. The government, becoming distrustful of its own reforms, rapidly returned to a reactionary policy. This caused only more unrest among the population, and was followed by the assassination of the Czar "Liberator," Alexander II.

Alexander III (1881–94), who succeeded on his father's assassination, sought to arrest any liberalization, and doggedly strengthened the autocratic regime.

THE END OF THE RUSSIAN EMPIRE

During the tragic era between 1904 and 1917, the Romanov dynasty gradually fell apart and the Russian Empire came to an end. Weak and incompetent, Russia's last Czar, Nicholas II (1894–1917), was easily influenced by reactionary advisors. On their irresponsible advice he involved Russia first in the unpopular and senseless Russo-Japanese War in 1904–05. Defeat in that war strengthened the revolutionary movement which fed on general dissatisfaction within Russia, making revolution possible.

REVOLUTION—1905

A large percentage of the rural population moved to urban areas as Russia became more industrialized. Working under harsh conditions, with long hours and little pay, the workers were naturally receptive to radical ideas.

Nicholas I (1825–55) felt that serfdom was an evil, but considered abolishing it an even greater evil.

On Sunday, January 9, 1905, a crowd of workers gathered in the streets of St. Petersburg. Led by a priest, Georgy A. Gapon, and armed only with icons and pictures of Czar Nicholas II, they marched to the Winter Palace in order to petition the monarch for more democratic reforms to better the lot of the workers. The streets, however, were soon blocked off by police and army units. When the crowd refused to disperse, the soldiers opened fire, killing over 130 persons and wounding several hundred, among them many women and children.

Emperor Paul I was supposedly the son of Catherine the Great and Peter III. There is, however, some doubt as to whether or not Peter III was his parent. After the memoirs of Catherine the Great were made public, Nicholas I, who was the monarch at that time, had all the copies confiscated and burned, for fear that his claim to the throne might be questioned.

31

Thus was born the first Russian Revolution: a wave of riots, strikes, murders and peasant revolts followed. Russia's heavy losses in the Russo-Japanese War, coupled with the chaos following the "Bloody Sunday," brought forth a general strike forcing the government to grant a limited constitution, with a representative Duma (parliament) to be elected democratically. This meant the beginning of the end of Russia's unlimited autocracy, but even this failed to restore order in the land. It resulted only in the formation of several political parties. Those satisfied with the constitution formed the Octobrist Party; the liberals united into the Constitutional Democratic Party; while the left-wing revolutionaries, who were by no means content, decided to continue their battle for complete social reforms, calling themselves the Social Democrats. The latter organized the first "Soviets" (councils of workers) among the striking workers.

Within a short time, the government arrested the Soviets, and this stopped all insurrections of the Moscow workers. With the restoration of order, the reactionary regime of Nicholas II was reinforced; the short-lived liberties were liquidated. But by now even the most ruthless government methods were unable to turn back a mounting tidal wave of revolution.

WORLD WAR I

As relations with the Kaiser's Germany became worse, Russia was forced into a Triple Entente with England and France, which inevitably drew Russia into World War I.

At the outbreak of World War I, most of the political parties joined in supporting Russia's effort, with the exception of the Bolsheviks, the left wing of the Social Democratic Party. The immense loss of life, suffering, and severe food shortage, both at the front and among civilians, created a "climate" for revolution.

The inept Czar, strongly influenced by his German-born wife, Empress Alexandra Feodorovna, and by her advisor, the sinister monk Gregory Y. Rasputin, as well as the entire cabinet, was soon suspected of secret dealings with Germany. All parties now withdrew their support of the monarchy. Revolutionary terror, strikes, propaganda and assassinations followed,

The Petrograd demonstration by workers and soldiers in 1917, was peaceful until the Provisional Government troops opened fire on the demonstrators.

One of the rare photographs of Vladimir I. Lenin in his Kremlin study, which has been preserved in the exact order that Lenin left it on his death—even the date on the calendar remains the same.

and futile attempts by the government to introduce agrarian reforms came to nothing.

MARXISM-LENINISM

The ideology of the Bolsheviks, later called Communists, was based on the socialist writings of a German, Karl Marx (1818–83). Certain changes were made by the Bolshevik leader and founder of the Russian Communist Party, Vladimir Ilyich Ulyanov who called himself Lenin.

Marxism was one of many schools of socialism which emerged in Western Europe as a result of the misery that accompanied the industrialization of Europe. Forecasting a violent, sudden revolution by the proletariat (working class), Marx urged the workers to seize power and use it for their own benefit. Marx based his theory on three "laws of history." He believed that all human institutions—

from art and religion to society and government—are determined primarily by economic conditions. To him, history was a "dialectic" process, by which he meant a series of struggles between opposing economic groups: the wealthy and the poor. Third, he believed in the inevitability of Communism. He said that the class struggle would result in one final upheaval, making the proletariat victorious over a defeated bourgeois (middle) class.

He predicted the "dictatorship of the proletariat"—a classless society in which the industrial workers would direct all the people. Lenin was Marxism's advocate in Russia, and his small group of Bolsheviks were looking for the right moment to create a revolution in which they could seize power.

REVOLUTION—1917

In February, 1917, the workers of Moscow and Petrograd (St. Petersburg until 1914) went

On the night of November 7, 1917, the Winter Palace, where the Provisional Government was in session, was stormed by the Bolsheviks, along with workers and sailors. Following an intensive battle, the Provisional Government was arrested. Its President, Alexander F. Kerensky, managed to escape, disguised as a woman.

out on strike, demanding higher food rations. The government replied by ordering the soldiers to open fire on the strikers. Mutiny spread in the army like wildfire, and the soldiers refused to fire, joining the ranks of the striking workers. After the fall of Petrograd to the insurgents, the Duma, which Nicholas attempted to dissolve, forced him to abdicate. A temporary Provisional Government was appointed. Nicholas and his family were imprisoned and finally, on July 16, 1918, they were executed in a cellar by the Bolsheviks.

Badly organized for war, and cut off now from its allies, Russia suffered immeasurably. The Provisional Government under Prince Lvov and later under Alexander Kerensky tried in vain to continue the war, only to be met by strong opposition from the soldiers and workers.

On November 6 and 7, 1917, the Bolsheviks, under the leadership of Lenin, seized control of the government with the aid of sailors and workers who stormed the Winter Palace in Petrograd, and captured the key buildings.

A peace treaty was concluded by the Bol-sheviks at Brest-Litovsk on March 3, 1918. In the bloody Civil War that followed between the so-called White and Red (Bolshevik) forces, the Reds emerged in 1920 as victors. Poland, Lithuania, Latvia and Estonia became independent, and until World War II they formed a "Quarantine Belt" between Soviet Russia and Western Europe.

Lenin moved the government back to Moscow in 1918 and changed the party name from Bolshevik to Communist. By 1922, Russia was reunited with the Ukraine, Byelorussia, and the Transcaucasian (Georgia, Armenia and Azerbaijan) Republics, which had broken away, and officially proclaimed itself the Union of Soviet Socialist Republics or the USSR. In 1924, Uzbekistan and Turkmenia were formed and added to the Union.

Lenin, together with Leon Trotsky and Josef Stalin, his comrades in the Communist party, turned attention to the land, devastated from end to end by years of war and revolution, in an attempt to put the country back on its feet as quickly as possible.

34

THE RISE OF THE USSR

Russia emerged from the Civil War in a state of collapse unequalled in modern history. The economic system was crumbling. The entire industrial system, burdened by a cumbersome management plan, was coming to a halt. Agriculture was reduced to a level far below the requirements of the nation. And yet, Russia as a nation endured, but at a terrible price of human life and suffering.

Russia pursued an economic policy called "War Communism," as an emergency measure during the course of the Civil War. Under this policy all trade and industry were nationalized by the government, grain and wheat requisitioned by force, and all financial capital confiscated. This resulted in a continuing decline of agriculture and industry, which was rapidly leading the country to total impoverishment. The drought of 1920 and 1921 led to a nationwide famine; 5,000,000 people lost their lives, twice as many as Russia's total casualties in World War I. The death toll would have been higher still had it not been for the assistance of the United States. In August, 1922, the United States fed more than 10,000,000 Russians daily and distributed an enormous quantity of medical supplies.

Public unrest, followed by the insurrection of the Kronstadt garrison, forced Lenin to introduce the New Economic Policy (NEP) in 1921, which allowed for a return to a limited capitalist system, although the basic policy of the Russian Communist party had always called for complete socialism. Private ownership of small business was permitted, private trade restored and the forced collectivization of grain was discontinued. (As a result of NEP, by 1928 the national income of the USSR reached above its pre-war level.) Overwhelmed with practical problems which affected the very existence of the state, and which demanded immediate solutions, the government proceeded first to consolidate Communist power within the country. Basic political plans and procedures were announced and efforts were made in the years 1921–24 to establish them, though without much success.

JOSEF STALIN

Lenin's death in 1924 was followed by a fierce struggle for power between Stalin and Trotsky. This political match was won by Stalin, whose main concern was to strengthen and consolidate Communism in Russia, and by this provide a gradual transformation of the society. He called this "Socialism in One Country." Trotsky, on the other hand, was impatient to realize his ideal of immediate Communist world revolution through what he called the process of "Permanent Revolution." Trotsky was later exiled from the Soviet Union. He settled in Mexico, where he was murdered in 1940.

It was under Stalin that the first Five Year Plan was introduced, when it became apparent that NEP would be inadequate for the country's future economic growth. Gradually the state managed to gain control of all aspects of life from politics to culture, education and public information.

The assassination on December 1, 1934, of Sergei M. Kirov, political leader of Leningrad and one of Stalin's most trusted aides, unleashed a series of purges against thousands of military

"Winter Palace Taken," was painted by Valentin A. Serov (1865–1911), an outstanding artist and a master portrait painter. Most of his work is now housed in Moscow's Tretyakov Gallery and the Hermitage Museum in Leningrad.

The two monuments on the sides of Dorogomilovsky Bridge in Moscow were erected to commemorate those who died defending Moscow against the armies of Napoleon in 1812 in the battle of Borodino. This is how the bridge looked in 1928.

and political leaders, lasting from 1936 to 1938. An alleged plot against Stalin had supposedly been uncovered, involving such Communist leaders as Trotsky and Marshal Mikhail N. Tukhachevsky, and many of Lenin's closest comrades-in-arms, such as Grigory Y. Zinoviev and Lev B. Kamenev. Russia's heavy losses later in World War II were caused in part by the fact that most of the army's best and most experienced leaders had fallen victim to the purges. Some were executed, while others were sent to work camps.

FOREIGN POLICY

Keeping the nation out of war has been the main objective of the Soviet government's foreign policy ever since the 1920's. As the "outcasts" of Europe after World War I, Russia and Germany concluded a co-operation accord at Rapallo, Italy in 1922. Most Soviet leaders realized that any attack against it by a

major power was likely to result in complete economic and political destruction of the USSR. Co-operation with Germany continued, despite Hitler's rise to power. When the Western powers failed to invite the USSR to negotiate with Hitler at Munich (1938), the Soviet Union concluded a non-aggression pact with Germany in 1939. Hitler's attack on Poland brought France and England into war with Germany. The USSR temporarily continued its pro-German policy and with Germany partitioned Poland by occupying all its territory up to the Bug River. At the same time, the Soviet Union annexed the Baltic States of Latvia, Lithuania and Estonia, making them into republics of the USSR by 1940. Russia invaded Finland in 1939 and waged war during the bitter winter into 1940. The Finns withstood the attack and obtained a Russian withdrawal after ceding Karelia and allowing the establishment of Russian military bases.

WORLD WAR II

Despite the non-aggression pact with Germany, there were growing signs that Hitler intended to invade the Soviet Union. The USSR grew apprehensive, and with good reason: Germany attacked on June 22, 1941. Kiev fell, as the German armies overran most of the Ukraine and Byelorussia. By 1941 Leningrad was surrounded. During a 29-month siege, some 3,000,000 heroic inhabitants of Leningrad withstood starvation, and more than 600,000 died.

A bitter winter, and a determined Russian counter-offensive saved Moscow. But the city of Stalingrad (later renamed Volgograd) was totally destroyed in 1942–43 during one of the most decisive and agonizing battles in all history. This served as a turning-point of the war, with nearly 330,000 German troops surrendering. Then, with a steady, unyielding offensive, the Soviet troops pushed into Poland and the Balkan Peninsula, liberating as they went. Finally on May 2, 1945, they marched through the streets of Berlin, and five days later, together with the Western Allies, accepted Germany's official surrender. Russia had paid a high price for victory, with a loss of millions and millions of lives.

The USSR declared war on Japan on August 8, 1945. Within a month, the Soviet forces penetrated deeply into Korea and Manchuria before Japan surrendered on September 2, 1945. As a result of the war and Allied agreements at Teheran, Yalta and Potsdam, the USSR gained the following territories: the Kuriles and the southern half of Sakhalin Island from Japan; some additional territory from Finland; and the northern territory of Eastern Prussia from Germany. The areas of the Ukraine and Byelorussia were greatly increased.

Today the Dorogomilovsky Bridge's name has been changed to Borodinsky Bridge. Below the waters of the Moscow River is the world's deepest underground transit station, the Kievskaya-Koltsevaya.

"Socialist Revolution Triumphed!" by B. Ioganson, is one of the few recent (1957) paintings in the government-sponsored Socialist Realism style, which strikingly resembles the style developed in Mexico in the public murals celebrating the revolutionary triumph of the lower classes. The revolutions in both countries took place during the same era.

THE COLD WAR

With the end of World War II, the USSR and the United States emerged as the two leading world powers. However, their co-operation and friendly relationships soon began to cool, and finally deteriorated into the "Cold War." The Western world became apprehensive over the increasing influence of the Soviet Union over Poland, Czechoslovakia, Hungary, Rumania, Bulgaria, Albania and mainland China, fearing the unlimited expansion of Communism. The Soviet Union was equally afraid that the Western powers would surround it. The relationship with the West went from bad to worse, finally erupting into hostilities when the United Nations beat back Communist forces in Korea in 1950–53.

The severity of the Cold War varied. At times Soviet-American relations seemed to warm, as during 1959, when Vice-President Richard Nixon journeyed to the American exhibition in Moscow, or during 1962–63, the last year of President Kennedy's administration.

But there were deep and continuing crises, many of which revolved round West Berlin, which is located far inside the territory of the East German Communist state. During the post-war period, the Russians attempted to blockade Berlin (1948–49), causing the Western Allies to mount a life-saving airlift to the troubled city. On various occasions the USSR threatened to end unilaterally Berlin's status as a city occupied by the wartime allies. On August 13, 1961, the East Germans frightened the West by erecting the notorious Berlin Wall, which sealed off the eastern section of the city from the American, British and French sectors.

Another crisis came in November, 1956, when the Soviet Union rushed troops into Hungary to quell a swelling anti-Communist revolt by Hungarian "Freedom Fighters." A decade later, hostilities again erupted over United States involvement in Vietnam.

THE KHRUSHCHEV ERA (1953-64)

Stalin's death (March 5, 1953) came as such a shock that top government officials warned the people against panic and disorder. "Collective leadership" was proclaimed with Nikita S. Khrushchev becoming the party chief, and Georgi M. Malenkov, the premier. Later Khrushchev assumed both positions after successfully defeating an opposition movement called the Anti-Party Group in 1957 and side-tracking his rivals.

The people of the Soviet Union began to gain more personal freedom and security. Under Khrushchev's leadership, the famous 20th Communist Party Congress ushered in a "de-Stalinization" campaign, and altered Communist theory to permit "peaceful co-existence" of nations with different social systems and the possibility of peaceful transition from "bourgeois democracy" to "Socialism." At the same time it continued a definite economic, diplomatic and psychological offensive abroad, especially in underdeveloped nations. It also startled the world with the launching of the first artificial satellite (or sputnik), on October 4, 1957, and subsequent space launchings of human beings. It alarmed the world with the testing of atomic bombs.

BREZHNEV AND KOSYGIN

The era came to an end on October 15, 1964, when Khrushchev was replaced as head of the Communist Party by Leonid I. Brezhnev and as Premier by Aleksei N. Kosygin, in a peaceful coup. On the domestic front, a new approach to government soon became evident. The government leaders denounced through the press Khrushchev's "subjective and emotional" style of leadership, but reaffirmed previous Soviet policy. They reshuffled power among themselves and called for a return of "collective leadership," in contrast to the one-man rule which had emerged under Khrushchev. The Five Year Plan they announced on February 20, 1966, was considered by most Western observers to be much more realistic than any previous plan in the goals it set. This may be attributed to the fact that Kosygin himself is an economist.

Although Nikita Khrushchev (1894–1972) was ousted from his formerly powerful position, the effects of his policies will be felt for some time to come.

He is viewed by outsiders as a shrewd businessman. Although the Soviet Union is not expected to reduce its heavy industrial output, the future plans of the country include a definite increase in light industry, with a strong emphasis on consumer goods for the purpose of raising the standard of living.

On the whole, the leaders of the Soviet Union now make fewer public appearances at banquets and receptions and are much more formal than was Khrushchev, which also makes them much harder to approach.

In foreign policy they face some major problems: their relationship with China, their attitude towards Southeast Asia, and the difficulty of keeping the Eastern Communist countries of Rumania, Poland and Eastern Germany in hand. And last, but not least, their stepped-up support of the Arabs against Israel, such as sending arms and trained personnel to Egypt, has added greatly to the danger in the Middle Eastern situation.

Towards the West they have tried to show more patience, wisdom and understanding and although "imperialism" is still being attacked, the slogans predicting World Communism have all but disappeared.

In August 1970, Russia signed a treaty with West Germany, in which both parties agreed to use only peaceful means in settling their mutual problems.

In 1972, relations with the West improved even more when the West German Parliament ratified this treaty, as well as a similar one with Poland.

In 1972, Russia and the United States made several unprecedented agreements regarding trade, space and ecology. Under the terms of the agreements, Russian wines were to be admitted to the United States, Pepsi-Cola would be sold in the Soviet Union, the two nations began joint studies of environment problems and plans began for a joint space flight to take place in 1975. Among the many commodities covered by the agreements, an important place was assigned to United States fertilizers to be used in Russian agriculture. This *détente*, or relaxation of tension, seemed to mark the beginning of a new era in Russo-American relations. Then in January, 1975, Russia repudiated the 1972 agreements, charging United States interference in Russian internal affairs. However, the historic link-up

in space of the Russian Soyuz and the United States Apollo in July, 1975, gave every appearance that *détente* was working in some respects.

Failure of the Russian wheat crop led to the purchase in 1972 of 30,000,000 bushels of wheat from the United States.

In 1973, new accords were signed between the two superpowers, covering oceanography (large-scale joint studies), agriculture (emphasis on research), transportation (joint projects with emphasis on cold-weather construction), and cultural exchange.

In 1975, a special plan, to end in 1990, was begun, to aid over-all economic development. The new plan cuts across political boundaries of the 15 republics, to create 7 large Planning Regions—North Central, South, Volga-Urals, Kazakhstan, Central Asia, Siberia and Far East.

CHINA

The USSR conflict with China has often been blamed on Khrushchev and his lack of subtlety in dealing with that country. Although there were differences between the two nations before, the open feud only started to appear towards 1959. Moscow's refusal to share atomic secrets with Peking in 1957 was one reason, but other issues involved a struggle for power, an ideological quarrel, and even territorial disputes.

Here a senior engineer is preparing the radio apparatus for contacting astronauts. Soviet scientists have developed some of the world's most advanced cosmic equipment. Soviet science considers the exploration of space of exceptional importance.

In the background of this view of the Palace Square in Leningrad is the General Staff Building, while the foreground is dominated by the graceful Alexander Column, erected to celebrate the victory of Russia over Napoleon in 1812.

3. GOVERNMENT

THE COMMUNIST PARTY

THE RULING POLITICAL ORGANIZATION in the USSR is the Communist Party of the Soviet Union (CPSU), the only legal political party in the country. In practice, major Soviet policies issue from its Central Committee, which instructs government and public organizations on how best to develop almost everything from the economy, to mass culture, to the needs of social welfare.

The Central Committee is the reigning body between sessions of the party's Congress which convenes, according to the Party Statutes, once every 4 years. The Congress brings together for a period of about 10 days to 2 weeks some 1,500 top Communists who are elected to represent the party's total membership, which now numbers about 14,000,000 (out of a population of 255,000,000.) It is the Congress which elects the Central Committee. Thus neither the Soviet people nor the mass of Communist members

The USSR is the most education-conscious country in the world after the United States, but the curriculum is rigidly supervised by the government. Although Russia can boast that there is virtually no uneducated citizen, free speech in public is definitely not encouraged.

have a direct say in its composition or its decisions.

Since the Central Committee is a body of about 300 members, and usually meets only two or three times a year, it, in turn, elects various bodies to direct and execute its policies on a day-to-day basis. These bodies are the Politburo and the Secretariat. The Politburo is composed of about a dozen members who are actively concerned with, and are ultimately responsible to the Central Committee for, developing policy. The Secretariat, also responsible to the Central Committee, is the party's chief executive arm. It is headed by a General Secretary who is, in fact, the Communist Party's chief, and who theoretically sits as an equal among equals on the Politburo.

GOVERNMENTAL ORGANS

Parallel to the Communist Party stands the vast governmental apparatus which conducts the nation's foreign and domestic policies, that is,

the policies developed within the Communist Party.

As in Western countries, the Soviet government may be divided into executive, legislative, and judicial branches whose authority is based on a constitution. The present constitution, which was written under Stalin, was adopted on December 5, 1936. It supplanted the previous constitutions of 1918 and 1924. The late Premier Khrushchev established a commission to formulate yet another constitution.

The highest legislative power is theoretically vested in the Supreme Soviet of the USSR, which meets about 10 days to 2 weeks every year to discuss and approve legislation. In practice, it amounts to a rubber stamp parliament and a dignified forum for open discussion of Soviet policies. Its debates are, on the whole, laudatory, although mild criticism is on occasion permissible.

The Supreme Soviet consists of two chambers—the Soviet or Council of the Union and the Soviet or Council of Nationalities. The former represents the interests of the entire Soviet people, while the latter expresses the special interests of the Soviet Union's many nationalities. The 1,517 Deputies of these two chambers are elected by universal suffrage for a period of four years.

It is a joint session of the two Chambers which formally names a Council of Ministers of the USSR, or cabinet, and designates the Chairman of the Council of Ministers or Premier. The Premier and his cabinet form the executive branch of the government.

A similar session names the Supreme Court of the USSR and appoints the country's Procurator General. The Supreme Court justices and the Procurator General head the Soviet judiciary which, of course, comprises an extensive system of lower courts and legal officers.

Since the Supreme Soviet assembles so infrequently, legislative matters which crop up between sessions are handled by a steering committee whose title is The Presidium of the Supreme Soviet. The chairman of this Presidium is deemed to be the chief of state, and his 15 deputies—one from each of the 15 Soviet republics—are considered, in Western terminology, to be Vice-Presidents of the Soviet Union.

Additionally, both chambers of the Supreme Soviet name committees to deal with various aspects of Soviet policy, and these meet from time to time to hold discussions on particularly important issues.

VOTING

Anyone over 18, male or female, can vote, and the minimum age for holding office is 23. Candidates for election may be nominated at factory meetings, collective farm gatherings, from trade unions or any other organization. A candidate need not be a member of the Communist Party, and once nominated he is assured election since he runs on a single slate, unopposed by any other candidate, in his constituency.

Soviet elections are always held on a Sunday and they take on the aura of a national holiday in which 99 per cent or more of the registered voters consistently turn out to cast their ballots for the single candidate. Of course, since the ballot is secret, voters can, and sometimes do, vote against the candidate. But in general, the candidate is elected by a huge proportion of the voters. Thus, in practical terms, the selective process in the Soviet election system ends with the nomination.

THE PRESS

The Soviet press—radio, television, and newspapers—are effectively controlled in the Soviet Union by the party and government authorities. In contrast to the part the press plays in Western democracies, the role of the press in the USSR is to inform the population on a carefully edited basis, to offer "inspired" criticism of social issues, and to mould public opinion to follow official policies.

POLITICAL DISSENT

The right to express disagreement with government policy has been denied consistently. Throughout the history of Soviet Russia, dissenters have been severely punished. Now, however, open dissent appears to be tolerated, at least when it comes from intellectuals and scientists. Whereas formerly, anyone who raised his voice in criticism was dealt with harshly, now only occasional scapegoats are punished. Formerly, a dissenter might receive 20 years in prison. Today, the sentence is much lighter, or may even take the form of brief commitment to a mental institution for "rehabilitation." In 1974, Aleksandr Solzhenitsyn, author of The Gulag Archipelago, which gave a grim picture of Soviet prison camps, was stripped of Soviet citizenship and deported, however. Another leading writer, Andrei Sakharov, awarded a Nobel Peace Prize in 1975, was officially censured.

(Left) These figure skaters are obviously taking their performance very seriously. This is the skating rink of the Young Pioneers' Stadium in Moscow.

(Right) A pupil displaying his model of a passenger rocket. On October 4, 1957, the Soviet Union launched its first Sputnik, thus ushering in the space era. The first man in space was Yuri A. Gagarin, and the first woman astronaut was Valentina V. Nikolayeva-Tereshkova.

Hunting is one of the popular sports of the country. In Siberia, this hunter is luring a stag.

Interior decorating varies from one region to the next. In northern Russia one can see houses decorated with fancy carvings, stocked with wooden utensils that have not changed in years. In the Ukraine, many houses are whitewashed, embroidered runners are the traditional decoration features, and the stoves are decorated with tiles portraying animals and plants. In the Caucasus and Central Asia, the main adornments consist of sheepskin rugs, beautiful pillows and carpets.

4. THE PEOPLE

THE PEOPLE of this multi-national country, with their varied traditions and customs, have made great contributions to world culture in ballet, music, literature, theatre and the fine arts. Although Russian is the official language of the country, the Soviet government has encouraged the many different nationalities to retain their heritage and language. Strangely enough, it is from these that some of the finest talent has emerged, despite the fact that only 30 years ago many of these ancient nationalities did not possess a written language.

LIVING CONDITIONS

What are the Russians like? Many foreigners find that the average Russian is quite similar to the average American. Both are hard workers, good providers and attached to their families. Russians display a genuine curiosity towards the foreigner and are known for their hospitality.

Living conditions have vastly improved in recent years, although the lack of consumer goods and living space is still a major problem.

Every town has its market known as the "Rynok." Most of the products there consist of fruits and vegetables. However, it is still quite difficult to buy fruit and vegetables out of season, and even if they are available their prices are exorbitant.

The average family usually has two bread-winners, but the lot of the woman is much harder than that of the man. Although both men and women enjoy professional respect and equality, the woman is still faced with all her household chores after working for 7 hours each day. Frequently the "babushka" (grandmother) helps out. However, there is no feeling of insecurity under the system, because the education of children is free and so is medical care. Therefore, there is no pressure to save money, a great deal of which is spent on food. If a person becomes ill he may receive either all, or at least 75 per cent of, his salary. Life in the rural areas is considerably more difficult, but even there, as industrialization penetrates deep into the country, both culture and living standards are rising rapidly.

Young Russians are especially conscious of modern trends and furnish their homes very simply, but with good taste.

Most nomadic tribes have settled down only in recent years. Not long ago they roamed the wide open country, hunting and living in tents.

Almost all Russian restaurants close at 11 o'clock with the exception of some found in Moscow, which stay open till 2, due largely to the demand of the tourists.

A lively Georgian national dance is performed by an amateur group of pupils in Batumi, Georgia. Folk dances and fairy tales of the Soviet Union are among the most sophisticated, intricate and charming in the world.

Many of the nationalities still retain their delightful folk costumes. Gaiety and song mark frequent country outings.

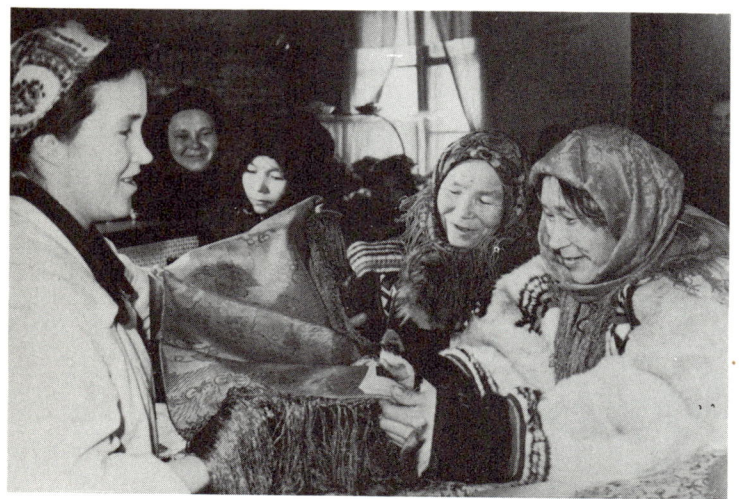

Women are incurable bargain seekers, whether in New York, Rome or at a rural shop in the Nenets National Region, beyond the Arctic Circle.

Most Russian children are
put into nurseries and
kindergartens since almost
all Russian women work.
Children may be left there
for a day or a week if
necessary.

The curriculum of
secondary schools covers
general knowledge of all
subjects, and technical as
well as on-the-job training.

The saying "A woman's
work is never done,"
illustrates well the life of
the average Russian
woman, who not only works
full time, but is expected to
carry out all the other
functions of a wife, mother
and homemaker. Shopping
for groceries in the crowded
"Gastronom" is a chore in
itself.

During the Stalin period Russian women were officially reproached if they attempted to look too feminine, because they were "wasting valuable time." Today, although it may cost half her monthly salary, the woman living in a large city will sport the latest spike-heeled shoes or an elegant Italian knit suit. Here is the interior of GUM, Moscow's State Department Store.

Chess is a popular national pastime and both young and old play the game with great enthusiasm. The world's leading chess players are usually Russian.

Although a Soviet citizen is not permitted to own land, he may nevertheless build his own house and upon his death it may be inherited by his heirs. A person may even will his possessions to someone residing outside the Soviet Union.

TRANSPORTATION

The people of the USSR do an unusual amount of travelling within their own country. Many are those who have been North, South, East and West in this mighty land. Travelling is fairly cheap, so almost no Soviet citizen stays home during his vacation. Children are sent by the trainloads to the Crimea and the Black Sea coast for a summer holiday, while their parents are free to travel where they will. Many people travel because of their work as well.

The most popular way to travel is still by rail. There are not many highways in the USSR that could accommodate a cross-country traveller, although more are being built. The city-to-city motorcoaches are rapidly gaining in popularity. For speed there is still nothing to top planes, which are inexpensive. In spite of these relatively modern means of travel, one of the best ways to see the USSR today is by using its ancient river routes. The rivers convey over 134,000,000 passengers annually, not to speak of commercial cargo.

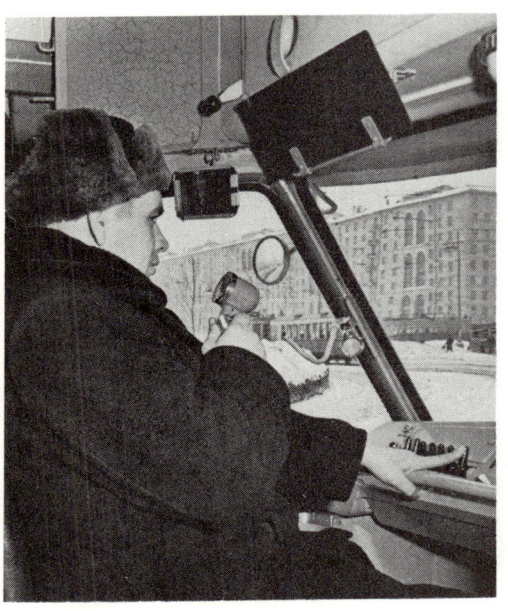

In the Moscow trolley-buses, the passengers all enter in the rear, put five kopeks in a coin-receiver, and extract a ticket. Most of the passengers do not try to cheat the government, but on occasion an inspector may enter the bus asking to see everyone's tickets. If by chance the passenger fails to produce one, he is fined 50 kopeks, not to speak of the embarrassment it causes him.

Because of the shortage of manpower after World War II, many jobs had to be taken over by women. Therefore it is not surprising to find women street-cleaners, bus and taxi drivers, doctors and engineers.

alphabet. Georgian and Armenian both have ancient alphabets of their own, which are quite different from the Latin and Cyrillic.

EDUCATION

All schools in the Soviet Union are run by the State. Secondary schooling at present is divided into two stages. All pupils are required to finish eight years of primary school, after which they may either go on to a secondary education, or enter a technical or trade school. They may also go to work and study in the evenings.

In higher education there exist three main divisions: full-time day study, evening study, and correspondence study. The degrees conferred by any of these three carry equal weight. Students in the secondary and higher schools receive government stipends or scholarships on which they live, since the education itself is free. If a student excels in his work he is rewarded by receiving 25 per cent above his regular stipend.

LANGUAGE

The languages of the Soviet Union belong to many different families and are written in different alphabets. Russian, Byelorussian, Ukrainian, Latvian, Lithuanian, Armenian and Tadzhik are Indo-European tongues. Estonian and many minor languages are related to Finnish, while Uzbek, Kazakh, Kirghiz, Azerbaijani and the various Tartar dialects are akin to Turkish. In addition, there are many smaller groupings, such as the Caucasian family, which includes Georgian.

The Cyrillic alphabet is used by the greatest number of people. However, Latvian, Lithuanian, Estonian and several of the Central Asian languages are written in the Latin

The Russian, Byelorussian, and Ukrainian languages employ the Cyrillic alphabet. This sign in Russian over the entrance of a department store in Leningrad says, "We invite you into our store."

Nearly 7,000,000 pre-school children spend their day in nurseries and kindergartens, and the demand for more nurseries is continually increasing.

RELIGION

Most Russians belong to no church, and in fact atheism is strongly advocated by the Communist Party. Of the few who are religious, the denomination with the largest number of adherents is the Russian Orthodox Church. The second largest denomination is Islam; there are also Roman Catholics, Lutherans, Evangelical Baptists, and a number of Jews. Buddhists can be found in many parts of the Asian USSR.

The state does not finance the church in any way, nor is religion taught in schools. The church and clergy have to depend on their own sources of income or on donations from their congregations. The teaching of religious beliefs by the clergy is also limited by the state.

Although many churches and places of worship have been open to the public for some time, the majority of those attending are old men and women. The younger generation has not been brought up to believe in God and therefore tends to view religion with a mixture of cynicism and amazement. However, on big religious holidays there is always a crowd of curiosity-seekers, especially during the beautiful Easter services.

In recent years, the problems faced by Jews in Russia have become acute. The Jews, numbering 3,500,000, have more limitations placed upon them than have Christians and Moslems. Though they are officially classed as a "nationality," they are not allowed to use Yiddish and Hebrew, while Ukrainians, Armenians and most other minorities may use their own languages. Many Jews would emigrate to Israel, if allowed—but only a handful have so far been able to leave. Complicating the situation is Russia's official support of the Arab states against Israel.

YOUTH

Virtually every boy and girl between the ages of 9 and 15 is a member of the Young Pioneers. These groups engage in a wide variety of activities which teach the youngsters to have a healthy respect for work, use their initiative, organize socially useful activities and be happy and courageous. Youngsters have at their disposal thousands of clubs, palaces, stadiums,

Early introduction to acting teaches and stimulates the children to love and respect the theatre. Plays are produced in 45 languages in the USSR's more than 500 professional theatres.

libraries, and camps. Most of these children later join the Young Communist League, a youth organization which is mainly concerned with the political education of the future citizens of the Communist State. It tries to instill in them the moral principles and ideals of the Communist society.

(Left) Maxim Gorky, shown here with his son Maxim, was a member of the Social Democratic Party. He helped Lenin raise funds for the Bolshevik faction of the party.

(Right) Nationally minded, Peter I. Tchaikovsky was not one of the "Kutchka"—the Big Five: Alexander P. Borodin (1833–87), Cesar A. Cui (1835–1918), Mily Balakirev (1836–1910), Nikolai A. Rimsky-Korsakov (1844–1908) and Modest P. Musorgsky (1839–81) — who looked upon Michael Glinka as a spiritual leader. However, Tchaikovsky was Russia's first well-known composer, and his soaring, lyrical works are among the most popular in the world.

(Left) Modest P. Musorgsky (1839–81) was perhaps the most original of Russia's "Big Five" composers. His famous piano composition, "Pictures at an Exhibition," is well constructed but unfortunately his lack of formal training is apparent in many of his works. Much of his life was spent working on his great opera, "Boris Godunov."

Ballet star Rudolf Nureyev took a record 89 curtain calls with Dame Margot Fonteyn in the Vienna State Opera House in one of Nureyev's first appearances after his defection from the USSR. Russia has produced many of the world's best ballet dancers, and some of the loveliest and most enduring ballet music. The Bolshoi ballet plays to a full house, whether in Russia or on tour throughout the world.

MUSIC

Although Peter the Great and Catherine the Great brought European music to Russia in the 18th century, the real father of Russian music was Michael I. Glinka (1804–57). He was the first to use folk and even Oriental elements in his works, which were not mere imitations of Western music. Subsequently Alexander Borodin, the prolific Nikolai Rimsky-Korsakov, Modest Musorgsky, and Peter I. Tchaikovsky (1840–93) developed some of the world's best-loved music.

LITERATURE

Despite the fact that Russian literature did not appear on the European scene until the middle of the 19th century, its tradition is quite long, dating back to the 11th century. However, the first really exciting literary figure was Russia's greatest poet, Alexander S. Pushkin (1799–1837). Deeply imbued with the spirit of classicism, he had a literary genius that managed to withstand the test of time. He was the first to fuse together successfully the spoken and the literary languages, which up to that time had

The great Russian painter, Ilya E. Repin, with his family. Among his famous canvases are "Ivan the Terrible Kills His Son Ivan" and the exuberant "Zaporozdzy Cossacks."

been totally different. He is the author of *Boris Godunov*, Russia's first national drama, and *Eugene Onegin*, one of the greatest verse novels.

Another great writer of the 19th century was Fyodor M. Dostoyevsky (1822–81), whose novels explored different stages in the development of psychology and philosophy, uncovering the hidden nature of man. Some of his best-known novels are: *The Brothers Karamazov, The Idiot*, and *Crime and Punishment*. Ivan S. Turgenev (1813–83) devoted much attention to the description of nature and the peasants. Later he concentrated on Russia's social conditions and changes, and was the first Russian writer to become acclaimed in the West. A member of the school of realism, Count Leo N. Tolstoy (1828–1910) is rightly considered to be the greatest Russian novelist of the 19th century. In his world-renowned novels *War and Peace* and *Anna Karenina*, Tolstoy not only recaptured "reality" most convincingly, but showed great insight into the human heart and mind. A fascinating writer with great universal appeal was Anton P. Chekhov (1860–1904), whose short stories and plays enjoy a great deal of popularity.

The Soviet period is enriched by the overpowering figure of Maxim Gorky (whose real name was Aleksei M. Peshkov) (1868–1936), often called the "father of Soviet literature." Although he started as an Impressionist, his later attraction for minute detail earned him the title of "the greatest master of Socialist Realism," a style created under Stalin's inspiration in the late Twenties. In practice it called for works which would serve to educate and instill party viewpoints in a mass audience. In literature this meant that it had to be socialist in content and realistic in form. Michael A. Sholokhov's great epic, *And Quiet Flows the Don*, amazing in its broad grasp of life, dramatic intensity, and the

Alexander S. Pushkin, whose black-skinned grandfather was an Ethiopian page of Peter the Great, is considered the father of Russian poetry and a master of prose and drama. Tragically, he died at the age of 38 in a duel.

This exquisite wash bowl and pitcher are the work of a 17th-century craftsman. Many indescribably lovely works of art were the possessions of the rulers of Russia.

simple and honest portrayal of its complex characters, won the Nobel Prize for Literature in 1965.

Poetry as an art form has had the most freedom of all artistic expressions in the USSR. The futurist poet Vladimir V. Mayakovsky (1893–1930) attained the highest poetic skill of the century, leaving a strong imprint on the work of his disciples. Among other Russian poets are Anna A. Akhmatova (1888–1966) and the late Boris L. Pasternak (1890–1960), whose novel, *Dr. Zhivago*, angered Soviet officialdom because of its deeply critical passages, and who was pressured to reject the Nobel Prize for Literature in 1958. Current poets include Andrei A. Voznesensky, Yevgeny A. Yevtushenko, and Bella A. Akhmadullina.

ART

Russian art is virtually unknown in the West, with the exception of the beautiful icons. After Russia's conversion to Christianity, iconography was almost the only form of painting Russia knew, up to the 16th century. Russian classicism developed under the guidance of Catherine the Great and many fine painters emerged at that time. The reign of Czar Nicholas I brought with it the development of Romantic painting.

The movement that followed was that of Russian Impressionism which lasted until 1920. Soon, however, it was replaced by a new group which called itself "Mir Iskusstva," formed by Serge P. Diaghilev, Alexander N. Benois, and Leon N. Bakst. They believed in "art for art's

These exquisite gold filigree medallions, with garnets and enamel, were found in the 19th century, and are the rarest discovery of Russia's early art form.

Wearing his traditional costume, a teacher engages in the ancient art of archery. Almost everyone in Russia engages in some form of sports activity.

"Kuresh" is a national wrestling game of Kirghizia. Every republic has its own particular sport, reflecting a variety of cultural influences.

Soccer is the number one form of sports entertainment, with nearly 15,000,000 spectators a year filing into the grandstands.

One of the most exciting sports to watch is the daring motorcycle race on ice.

This is the main arena of the Lenin Stadium in Moscow. The pride and joy of sports-loving Muscovites, it is pointed out to tourists as one of the seven wonders of the modern world.

sake" and quickly formed ties with the West. During the Soviet period the style of Socialist Realism was officially adopted. This called for the creation of a "positive hero" and resulted in a great deal of portrait painting.

Today, Russia has become more exposed to modern, Western art. For the past few years, young artists have produced many fine paintings, most of which are abstract and non-objective, showing an amazing freedom of expression and vitality. Though many of them have not been officially exhibited and do not earn the approval of the USSR's Artists Union, these paintings are slowly emerging from the "closets," and can be seen. Some of the leading figures are Yury Vasilyev, Dmitri Krasnopevtsev, and Ilya Glazunov.

SPORTS

The people of the USSR are ardent sport enthusiasts and if they do not participate in a sports activity themselves, they readily enjoy being spectators.

Although officially there are no professional sports in the USSR, most of the athletes cannot really consider themselves amateurs either. Their training is severe, demanding much time and energy, and a great deal of assistance comes from the government, both financial and moral. In fact, many of the leading athletes want to be called professionals, because they feel this would be a much more realistic appraisal. The most popular sport is soccer and both young and old fill the grandstands when there is a match.

Since 1952 Soviet sportsmen have participated in the Olympic Games, coming away every time with some of the gold medals after setting new records. Russia's women athletes are considered the best in the world. All in all, nearly 5,000,000 people participate in light athletics, 4,000,000 play volleyball, almost 4,000,000 ski, more than 3,000,000 enjoy football and about 1,000,000 are gymnasts.

(Left) A student returning to his former place of work for a visit is being shown the additions to the plant by an old hand. Many workers are being encouraged to improve their knowledge by entering specialized technical schools. Soviet workers are encouraged to overfulfil their required quota and are rewarded, in certain fields, with bonuses and pay rises.

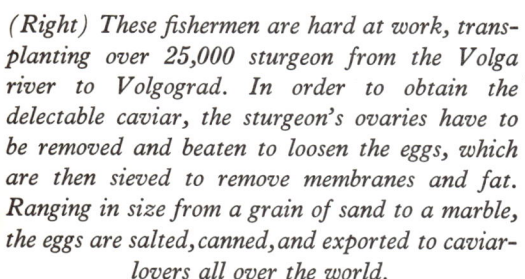

(Right) These fishermen are hard at work, transplanting over 25,000 sturgeon from the Volga river to Volgograd. In order to obtain the delectable caviar, the sturgeon's ovaries have to be removed and beaten to loosen the eggs, which are then sieved to remove membranes and fat. Ranging in size from a grain of sand to a marble, the eggs are salted, canned, and exported to caviar-lovers all over the world.

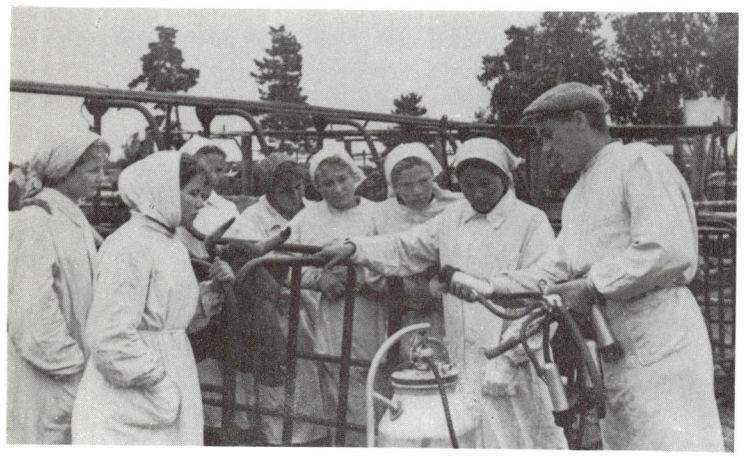

Students who are planning to specialize in agriculture are undergoing training at a collective farm in Kazakhskaya. In 1963 the USSR's cultivated land was 539,695,000 acres, and there were 9,200 state farms and 34,600 collective farms.

This house in Leningrad is being constructed from top to bottom, after the framework has gone up. Each section has been prefabricated, complete with space for wiring and pipes, before being lifted into place. The electricians and plumbers need only to connect the sections together after all are hoisted into position. It is easier to thread wires and pipes downward, and that is why the Russian workers start at the top.

5. ECONOMY

AFTER THE REVOLUTION of 1917, all private enterprise was abolished in the USSR, although the Communists met strong initial resistance. Today all the land, minerals, waters, banks, factories, mines, large agricultural enterprises, and most of the dwellings are State property, theoretically belonging to all the people collectively. Although a person may own a house, the land on which it is built belongs to the State. Since there is no private enterprise, in the Soviet Union all workers are employed by the government.

Today the country is operated on a basis of a planned economy. This enables the men who are in charge of production to concentrate a particular factory on one objective or to change it if necessary to another type of manufacture—something which is not done so easily in other nations. The current Five Year Plan was preceded by eight others. The first was put into operation in 1928, under Stalin, when it became obvious that NEP was delaying the formation of a state-operated, socialist economy. During the first three Five Year Plans, heavy industry and production of vitally needed equipment and raw materials were tremendously accelerated, resulting in a fantastic growth of both agriculture and industry in a few short years.

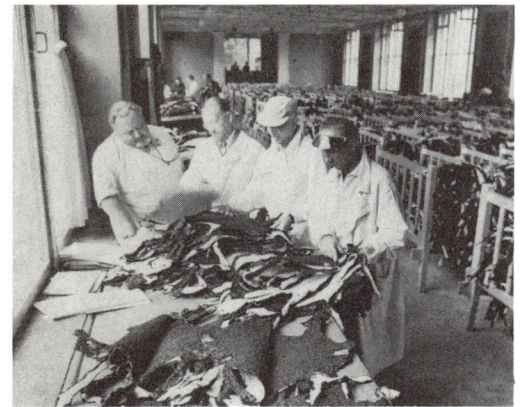

In the fourth Five Year Plan (1946–50) industrial production surpassed the pre-war level, although agriculture continued to suffer from lack of incentive among the peasants. The fifth Five Year Plan continued to stress heavy industry, but did increase consumer goods slightly. Replacing the over-estimated sixth Five Year Plan (1956–60) was the ambitious Seven Year Plan (1959–65), which called for accelerated housing construction, industrial output and a 40 per cent increase in the standard of living.

Announced in February, 1966, the blueprint of the eighth Five Year Plan stressed priority to consumer goods and emphasized agricultural production. The Soviet government had in effect promised its citizens better food and clothing, higher income (or lower prices), and more motor-cars and apartments by 1970; in short, a better material life.

However, Russia entered 1970, the last year of the 1966 Plan, with a slowed-down, rather than an expanding, economy. Housing was far more available, and television and radio sets abundant—but furniture, motor cars, and good clothing were hard to come by. Foreign observers blamed the slow-down on the failure of management to keep up with technological change.

The ninth Plan (1971–75) aimed for greater production of consumer goods, through improved management methods and increased mechanization.

In June, 1974, Russia and the United States signed a new 10-year pact, extending the 1972 trade agreement. This move reflected the growth of Russian trade with the West, which grew by

World-renowned for its squirrel, muskrat, sable, silver fox, mink and Persian lamb, the USSR ranks first in the world in the variety, quantity and value of its furs.

40 per cent in 1973, contrasted with a mere 9 per cent increase in Russian trade with the Communist bloc in the same period.

The ninth Plan's emphasis on consumer goods fell far short of its aims, due to continued crop failures. The tenth Plan (1976–1980) set as its goals expanded production of food, fuel and heavy machinery and equipment.

AGRICULTURE

With the introduction of the first Five Year Plan in 1928, collective farms were ruthlessly introduced throughout the country. With the land owned by the State, all smaller farms were forcibly collectivized and were then worked by the peasants together. In these farms the peasants have collective ownership of the basic means of production such as farm buildings, draught animals, livestock and farm machinery.

In recent years, Soviet agriculture has suffered numerous setbacks, largely due to harsh weather conditions. These forced the Kremlin to buy enormous quantities of grain abroad, particularly from the United States and Canada. However, other difficulties exist in the Soviet farming system which make for yields far below the potential. The greatest problems are a lack of widespread mechanization, and a lack of chemical fertilizers. Further, the previous organization of farm workers was inefficient and offered little incentive. Current changes in working conditions are aimed at overcoming these drawbacks. In March, 1965, Brezhnev announced a vast plan to invest very heavily in agriculture, and generally ease the financial situation with more generous credits. The Soviet government, revising working conditions on the collective farms, decided to introduce a guaranteed monthly wage for farmers. This went into effect on July 1, 1966, and replaced an earlier system of payment for the amount of work produced and its quality. Pensions were also introduced for the first time for collective farmers. The Soviet Union also has State Farms, which are state-operated and state-owned. The

Land, like all natural wealth, is considered state property, belonging to all the people. Agriculture, however, has for years been the weakest area of the USSR's economy. With modern methods and machinery the Soviet Union expects to secure better crops in the near future. Now, for the first time, the collective farm worker has been guaranteed a wage equivalent to that of a factory worker. This was done in the hope of luring and holding skilled workers, who often prefer to live in the city.

peasants do not own any part of these farms and are paid strictly in cash. In the countryside, an agricultural tax is collected on incomes from personal products grown on the small private plots allocated to each collective farmer.

INDUSTRY

The USSR accounts for over 20 per cent of the total world industrial production, which puts it in second place after the United States. Its main output is in heavy industry, mainly electrification, mechanization and automation of the economy. The USSR is the first in Europe and second in the world in the production of electric power. Until recently, coal dominated the Soviet Union's fuel balance, but because oil and natural gas are more expedient and far more convenient to use, the USSR has now emphasized priority in oil and gas extraction and processing. Under the long term plan (1961–80), gas output is to increase nearly 14 to 15 times and oil five times.

A large-scale chemical industry is rapidly being built up—the USSR stands second in the world already in its output of chemical products. A great deal has been done in the automation of production, and the possibilities for further automation and mechanization are endless. If workers are displaced, the State simply moves them to other jobs.

WORKING CONDITIONS

The average working week in the USSR is a little under 40 hours, with 36 hours for all persons working under unusually difficult conditions Wages depend on the worker's qualifications, as well as on the conditions under which he has to perform his job. Bonuses are given for over-fulfilling the quota, or if the finished product has in some way been improved by the worker—as well as for long years of service.

Women have full equality with men in almost any profession. They are often seen working as street cleaners, steam-roller operators and in steel mills. Expectant mothers are granted 3 months' paid leave when their child is about to be born. Almost all factories and offices have their own nurseries for the care of the children of the female employees. The rigorous climate, lack of conveniences and hard work often age

63

Baku is the capital of Azerbaijan, the land of "black and white gold." The white symbolizes the area's cotton crop, the black, oil. Derricks have appeared in the Kura Basin, on the foothills of the Caucasus Mountains and far out into the open sea. Known as the "City on Stilts," the Baku oil "field" extends 70 miles from shore. Shown here is a steel trestle, carrying the "black gold" from the Caspian Sea.

Russians more than their counterparts in the wealthier capitalistic countries. The retirement age in the Soviet Union is 60 for men, 55 for women. If a person does not wish to retire, he may continue to work on salary.

NATIONAL INCOME

The national income is distributed in the following way: Approximately one quarter is used for the enlargement and improvement of production, while 90 per cent of the remaining three quarters is distributed in the form of wages and for the construction of schools, apartments, hospitals, and scientific and cultural establishments.

The real income of the salary workers is rising. This is evident in the fact that the population bought 13 per cent more furniture in 1963 than in 1961, 33 per cent more cars, and 38 per cent more washing machines. The average family spends approximately 10 per cent of its earnings for rent, between 50 and 65 per cent on food, and a small percentage on entertainment, which is relatively inexpensive. Taxes in the Soviet Union make up only about 7 per cent of the total revenue. Individual income taxes range

anywhere from 0.1 to 13 per cent, depending on the number of dependents and salary. Owners of houses pay a house tax and land rent.

FINANCE

The bank notes or treasury notes of the USSR are called "rubles" and the coins are "kopecks." Most Westerners are surprised to find banks in the Soviet Union. Some local savings banks pay up to 3 per cent interest. Banking is a state monopoly and its chief function is to grant organizations short-term credits; receive and pay out money for the state budget account; arrange and settle international accounts, and exercise supervision over bank loans.

ECONOMIC PROGRESS

In certain sectors, Russia has made impressive advances in recent years. In 1971 and 1972, Soviet steel production surpassed that of the United States, to become the world's largest. In 1972, the Russian merchant marine replaced that of the United States as fifth largest in gross tonnage.